14
Scriptural Principles
for Daily Living
Vol. 1

14 Scriptural Principles for Daily Living Vol. 1

> "Your words are a flashlight to light the path ahead of me and keep me from stumbling."
> [Psalm 119:105 TLB]

Anthony Adefarakan

GLOEM, CANADA

Dedication

I dedicate this book to God Almighty for His goodness and faithfulness in making His Word available to me. All glory to His Holy Name.

Also to everyone desirous of a closer walk with God, living out His precepts on a daily basis, I am in agreement with you all and I decree that grace for a closer walk with God is coming upon you in Jesus' Name.

Acknowledgement

I sincerely acknowledge my Eternal Father, Who alone is the Source of all wisdom. He is the Author and Finisher of my faith and it is of His fullness that the contents of this book have been drawn.

Also, I want to profoundly appreciate my dear parents – Prince and Mrs. Timothy Adefarakan – for bringing me up in the way of the Lord and for instilling righteousness consciousness in me. The wonderful education foundation I was given, coupled with their constant encouragement has empowered me to reach heights that were once beyond my imagination.

My most special appreciation goes to my sweetheart, Abisolami; without her help and support I would never have enjoyed the conducive atmosphere needed to publish this book. I appreciate your love, encouragement, and the support you give at all times. Thank you so much. I love you my Baby!

And to all my mentors in Ministry, I appreciate you all. Your investments in my life are not in vain. May the Lord reward you all in Jesus' Name.

Introduction

Life on earth has been described as a form of pilgrimage with eternity as man's final destination.

1 Peter 2:11 TLB says:
"Dear brothers, you are only visitors here. Since your real home is in heaven, I beg you to keep away from the evil pleasures of this world; they are not for you, for they fight against your very souls."

And Hebrews 11:13 also says:
"These men of faith I have mentioned died without ever receiving all that God had promised them; but they saw it all awaiting them on ahead and were glad, for they agreed that this earth was not their real home but that they were just strangers visiting down here."

In the course of this brief earthly sojourn, we

are bound to face certain situations capable of generating questions like *'what step do I take?' 'where do I settle?' 'who do I marry?' 'will I be rich or poor?' 'how do I finance my projects?' 'how do I take good care of my family?' 'how do I know God's will for my life?'* just to mention a few. Usually, we find it difficult to provide correct answers to these questions due to our weak mortal nature.

However, there is a manual for this pilgrimage, which is the Word of God. The One Who designed this journey for us has put in the manual all we need to navigate our way successfully and to eventually end up on the glorious side of eternity when the pilgrimage is over. Little wonder David prayed in Psalm 119:19 – *"I am a stranger in the earth; hide not thy commandment from me".*

The principles presented in this book are all Bible-based and will deliver results every time they are applied because the Word of God is forever settled in Heaven (Psalm 119:89).

I pray as you read on, God's grace to apply these principles will rest upon you in Jesus' Name.

Anthony Adefarakan.

Principle #1

Divine Insurance Policy

Knowing Jesus Christ and accepting Him as your Lord and Saviour not only secures your eternal bliss in Heaven but also guarantees your security on earth. Jesus is the Best Insurance Policy you can sign up for while your earthly pilgrimage lasts.

A dictionary defines insurance as a practice or arrangement by which a company or government agency provides a guarantee of compensation for specified loss, damage, illness, or death in return for payment of a premium.

Going by this definition, it means the one insured or their beneficiary only gets to enjoy the benefits of the insurance if there is a loss, damage, illness or eventual death. That's how insurance policies work down here. You suffer a loss first, then you make claims to recover the loss or at least get through it.

But divine insurance doesn't work like that. When you sign up for this unique kind of insurance, you don't get to record losses before making claims; instead, you are supernaturally empowered to prevent or mitigate loss of health, wealth, property and even life.

You pay premiums to insurance companies in order to enjoy or keep enjoying their benefits; but in the case of this divine insurance policy, Jesus has already paid in full for all who will believe and put their trust in Him. All you need to start enjoying the benefits of this divine insurance is to accept the Lordship of the One Who paid the full premium over your life; and that's Jesus Christ. There is nothing difficult in that; is there?

Proverbs 18:10 NJKV says:
"The name of the LORD is a strong tower; The righteous run to it and are safe."

And Romans 10:13 also says"

"...whosoever shall call upon the name of the Lord shall be saved."

Connect with Jesus today and subscribe to this Divine Insurance Policy; He has no record of failures!

Principle #2

The Hope of Glory

Colossians 1:27 says *'....Christ in you, the hope of glory'*. Conversely, that scripture would be rendered as 'Christ not in you, the hope of shame'.

Eternal Glory is available as well as Eternal Shame, it all depends on where Christ is located in your life - in you or not in you.

It is the presence of the Spirit of Christ in a man that enables such a man to overcome sinful tendencies. When Christ lives in you, you are supernaturally empowered to live a life of holiness because the Spirit of Christ is holy.

But when Christ is not living inside of you, you will be exposed to all manners of sinful tendencies without any power to resist them. You will just notice you keep falling every time you are tempted to sin. And because Proverbs 18:3 GNT says *'Sin and shame go together...'* you can be sure shame is the only thing you can look forward to in the future.

Surrendering your life to Jesus Christ is the only guarantee you have to expect a glorious future. Isaiah 3:10 NKJV says *'Say to the righteous that it shall be well with them, For they shall eat the fruit of their doings.'*

To have Christ living in you assures you of eternal glory while to not have Him living in you assures you of eternal shame.

Christ is still knocking on the doors of people's hearts today. He says in Revelation 3:20 NKJV - *'Behold, I stand at the door and knock. If anyone hears My voice and opens the door, I will come in to him and dine with him, and he with Me.'*

Decide for glory today, and you will simply escape eternal shame.

Principle #3

What the Devil Fears

The devil is not afraid of your church titles, neither is he afraid of the grammar you blow when praying. There is only ONE thing he cannot stand in your life; that is THE KNOWLEDGE OF GOD AT WORK IN YOUR LIFE. And this knowledge comes from THE WORD OF GOD.

Look at the temptation of Jesus Christ in the wilderness as recorded in Matthew 4:1-11. Jesus had been fasting and praying for 40 days and 40 nights; that didn't scare the devil away from Him. He presented Him with three different dimensions of temptation and the only thing that got him off was the knowledge of the Word of God at work in Jesus (being the Word Himself).

To live a Wordless life is to be vulnerable to

satanic assaults with no defense whatsoever. The only thing that makes the devil tremble is the correct application of the Word of God. Revelation 12:11 says we overcame him by the Blood of the Lamb and by the Word of our testimony. Does it not surprise you that each time Jesus was tempted by the devil, He kept answering by saying *'it is written'*? If you don't know what is written, you are not a match for the devil. You must feed your heart with the Word of God and always get ready to use it skillfully whenever the devil comes at you with his wiles.

So to keep the devil where he belongs- under your feet, get to know Jesus and start doing whatever He tells you in His Word. That is the pathway to a life of dominion on this planet!

He said in John 8:31-32: *'If you continue in My word, then you are truly disciples of Mine; and you will know the truth, and the truth will make you free.'*
Free from what?
Free from all forms of satanic assaults.

ANTHONY ADEFARAKAN

Principle #4

The Helmet of Salvation

The writer of the epistle to the Ephesians described salvation as a helmet. Helmets are worn to protect the head from injuries, attacks and the likes. And the head is such an important part of the body such that even though it doesn't house the heart, once it is off, the entire body becomes lifeless.

As at this very second, arrows of darkness are flying about seeking careless victims. Our enemies are not physical beings; they are spiritual wicked forces with a mission to wreck untold havoc in the lives of God's children. They don't recognize physical helmets; they only recognize spiritual ones. So if they can't find any helmet on your head (which is your salvation), they simply go for your head and that can be very catastrophic.

Ephesians 6:10-18 NLT says:

"...Be strong in the Lord and in his mighty power. Put on all of God's armor so that you will be able to stand firm against all strategies of the devil. For we are not fighting against flesh-and-blood enemies, but against evil rulers and authorities of the unseen world, against mighty powers in this dark world, and against evil spirits in the heavenly places.

Therefore, put on every piece of God's armor so you will be able to resist the enemy in the time of evil. Then after the battle you will still be standing firm. Stand your ground, putting on the belt of truth and the body armor of God's righteousness. For shoes, put on the peace that comes from the Good News so that you will be fully prepared. In addition to all of these, hold up the shield of faith to stop the fiery arrows of the devil. Put on salvation as your helmet, and take the sword of the Spirit, which is the word of God.

Pray in the Spirit at all times and on every occasion. Stay alert and be persistent in your prayers..."

My candid advice to you is that you grab your helmet - by accepting the salvation Jesus offers, and your head will be protected. You will not lose your head in the battles of life in Jesus' Name.

Peace be with you!

Principle #5

Your Fellowship – His Priority

Mark 3:13-15 NKJV says:

"And He went up on the mountain and called to Him those He Himself wanted. And they came to Him. Then He appointed twelve, that they might be with Him and that He might send them out to preach, and to have power to heal sicknesses and to cast out demons:"

Your fellowship is more important to God than your services. In the Garden of Eden, it was said that Adam and Eve heard the sound of God walking in the cool of the day (Genesis 3:8). Apparently, He had come down to have some intimate moments with them.

If you also look at Luke 10:38-42 NLT, this matter of fellowship ahead of service played out.

"As Jesus and the disciples continued on their way to Jerusalem, they came to a certain village where a woman named Martha welcomed him into her home. Her sister, Mary, sat at the Lord's feet, listening to what he taught. But Martha was distracted by the big dinner she was preparing. She came to Jesus and said, "Lord, doesn't it seem unfair to you that my sister just sits here while I do all the work? Tell her to come and help me."

But the Lord said to her, "My dear Martha, you are worried and upset over all these details! There is only one thing worth being concerned about. Mary has discovered it, and it will not be taken away from her."

Martha was genuinely concerned about rendering certain services towards entertaining the Lord but Mary simply sat down and listened to Jesus, intimately fellowshipping with Him. And from the response of Jesus when Martha complained about being left alone to do all the serving, intimacy (fellowship) is of a higher priority to Him than our services.

Now, don't get it wrong. He wants your services too, but only after you have satisfied the fellowship part. That Mark 3:13-15 says He chose them that they might be with Him and that He might send them out. That is, they were primarily chosen for fellowship and secondarily for service. That order must be maintained at all times in order to keep your spiritual life on the right course.

If we put services ahead of fellowship, it's a matter of time, we will be totally drained out. That explains why a lot of Christians get stressed out over ministerial responsibilities. They have got the priority backwards. Refreshment as well as strength for effective service comes from a quality time of intimacy with the Lord of the work.

So, love not the Lord only on Sundays, He desires your fellowship every other day of the week. Take your time and carry the consciousness of His Presence into each new week He causes you to experience and you will be surprised at the result.

Jesus loves you and wants to have a daily fellowship with you. Will you let Him in?

Selah!

Principle #6

Emmanuel Always Sees

One of the other Names of Jesus Christ as prophesied by Isaiah in Isaiah 7:14 is EMMANUEL - meaning God with us. This means you are never alone because His Presence is everywhere you turn, so you can expect God's intervention always.

But it also means every sin you commit is not hidden from Him including the ones you carry out behind closed doors.

Hebrews 4:13 NIV says *"Nothing in all creation is hidden from God's sight. Everything is uncovered and laid bare before the eyes of him to whom we must give account."*

Everything that looks hidden from men is clearly visible before God. As a matter of fact,

Psalm 139:7-12 NIV paints the picture so clearly. It says:

"Where can I go from your Spirit?
Where can I flee from your presence?
If I go up to the heavens, you are there;
if I make my bed in the depths, you are there.
If I rise on the wings of the dawn,
if I settle on the far side of the sea,
even there your hand will guide me,
your right hand will hold me fast.
If I say, "Surely the darkness will hide me
and the light become night around me,"
even the darkness will not be dark to you;
the night will shine like the day,
for darkness is as light to you."

You see, that's why God's judgment is going to be very fair because He sees everything, even down to our very motives for doing what we do.

Watch the way you live, you can't really do without Christ because He is Emmanuel. And guess what? He is the One appointed by the Father to judge both the living and the dead. So, start living right beginning from now before you meet Him at the JUDGMENT SEAT.

Remember, Emmanuel always sees.

Principle #7

Experiencing the New

2 Corinthians 5:17 says *'... if any man be in Christ, he is a new creature: old things are passed away; behold, all things are become new'*. The reason many Christians don't experience newness of life is because they have refused to let the 'old' go. Until the old passes away, the new will not come.

Matthew 9:17 CEV says:
"No one pours new wine into old wineskins. The wine would swell and burst the old skins. Then the wine would be lost, and the skins would be ruined. New wine must be put into new wineskins. Both the skins and the wine will then be safe."

New wine must be put into new wineskins. You can't be in Christ and still be harboring grudges, malice, unforgiveness, hatred, bitterness, resentment, rebellion etc. Those are the old that you have to put away in order to embrace the new life in Christ Jesus.

You can't accommodate your sinful habits together with the righteousness of God in the same vessel. The old must pass away for the new to surface.

Let go of your old sinful habits and you will see a new you emerging. You are lifted in Jesus' Name.

Principle #8

Attitude of Gratitude

Gratitude has been defined as the quality of being thankful; readiness to show appreciation for and to return kindness. It is a warm feeling of thankfulness towards the world, or towards specific individuals.

The person who feels gratitude is thankful for what they have, and does not constantly seek more.

There is one scripture I love so much as far as this subject of gratitude is concerned. It is 1 Thessalonians 5:18 NLT; it says *"Be thankful in all circumstances, for this is God's will for you who belong to Christ Jesus."*

Did you see the word *'you'* in that verse? That means this scripture is not written for everybody;

it's for a particular category of people – those who belong to Christ Jesus. So it is the will of God for you to be thankful in all circumstances as a child of God even if no one around you is thankful.

Gratitude is a personal affair; you are to choose to be thankful even if your parents, spouse or pastors aren't. They may all be complaining, but you are to give thanks.

Now, why should we be thankful? There are at least three reasons.

Firstly, because God expects it. In Luke 17:17-18, after Jesus had instructed those lepers seeking to be cleansed on what to do, He remained on the same spot waiting for their gratitude. That's why He was so disappointed when only one out of the ten cleansed came back to thank Him. God is good; and for everything He does for you –sleeping and waking up, going out and coming in, breathing in and breathing out, shelter, protection, provision, grace, forgiveness, mercy among other benefits you enjoy from Him daily, He expects your gratitude.

Secondly, we should be thankful because we only know in part according to 1 Corinthians 13:9a. We don't always know the whole story. What appears to be a disappointment to you might actually be God's way of saving you from a major financial loss. That little delay you encountered might actually be His way of keeping you around for a bigger blessing. You don't and can't know all the story because you are not omniscient. That's why He expects your gratitude. He is always working with the bigger picture in mind; and remember, according to Romans 8:28, all things are working together for your good as long as you love Him and are still in His purpose. Learn to constantly remind yourself that God always works with your best interest at heart. That's enough reason to keep thanking Him.

And lastly, we should give thanks because that is His will for us according to 1 Thessalonians 5:18. Doing God's will is obedience which attracts

His blessings while not doing His will is disobedience which definitely attracts His judgment. So, to be thankful is to be obedient; and to be obedient is to escape His judgement.

You see, there is one major danger of ingratitude that I saw in Psalm 28:5 KJV. It says: *"Because they regard not the works of the LORD, nor the operation of his hands, he shall destroy them, and not build them up."*

From this scripture, it is crystal clear that anything you are not grateful for you are bound to lose. If you are not grateful for your health, expect sickness; if you are not grateful for your promotion, expect demotion; and if you are not grateful for your provision, expect lack. And according to that Psalm 28:5, God is the One who will do the destroying (tearing down), not the devil. It's a very dangerous thing to live an ungrateful life.

I have identified some indicators that can let you know whenever you are beginning to be ungrateful. When you start complaining, murmuring, grumbling or lamenting over anything including what others have that you do not have, you are entering the destruction zone of ingratitude. Every time you are complaining you are not being grateful; you can't do both at the same time.

Also, focusing only on what you feel God hasn't done instead of what He has done is an open invitation to ingratitude and its grievous consequences. Learn to look for things to thank God for even when everything and everyone around you keeps suggesting otherwise. Matthew 7:8 says everyone that seeks finds. If you look for reasons to be grateful, you will find more than enough.

Luke 19:26 NIV says *"...I tell you that to everyone who has, more will be given, but as for the one who has nothing, even what they have will be taken away."*

If you keep giving thanks, you will be given more reasons to be thankful; but if you remain ungrateful, the little things you should have been grateful for will be taken away from you. Beware!

Grateful people don't murmur neither do they complain, instead they give thanks for everything. And when situations seem to be getting out of hand, they simply trust God. That's how to live a grateful life.

Principle #9

Guard Your Heart

"How art thou fallen from heaven, O Lucifer...For thou hast said in thine heart, I will ascend into heaven, I will exalt my throne above the stars of God... I will be like the most High. Yet thou shalt be brought down to hell, to the sides of the pit." (Isaiah 14:12-15).

If you have ever wondered why Lucifer (the devil) was thrown out of heaven, that's why. Iniquity was found in his heart, and such cannot be accommodated in Heaven (God's Holy Dwelling Place).

Now, there is something very important I want to point out to you from that text. Lucifer had only said those things in his heart, he had not even carried them out, yet he was judged.

What lesson can we learn from that?

We have to consciously watch and pay attention to the content(s) of our hearts at every point in time. Once God sees a thing in your heart, He holds you responsible for it.

Jesus said mere looking lustfully at a woman qualifies one as an adulterer. Look at it in Matthew 5:28 NIV; it says *"But I tell you that anyone who looks at a woman lustfully has already committed adultery with her in his heart."*

You know the meaning of that? The same punishment that actual adultery attracts is what 'imagined adultery' also attracts. So whether you imagine it in your heart or you actually carry out the act, the judgment is the same because God sees the content of your heart the same way He sees your actions. Matthew 12:34 says from the abundance of the earth, the mouth speaks. So the content of your heart at every point in time is very important to God.

The devil only had it in his heart to be like the Most High before he was cast down. He had not even executed it yet. Guard your heart with all diligence!

Proverbs 4:23 NLT says *"Guard your heart above all else, for it determines the course of your life."*

Principle #10

The Imprisonment of Unforgiveness

A warder is defined as a prison guard whose primary responsibility is to ensure no prisoner escapes. But the challenge of a warder is this: as long as there are prisoners to look after, he himself remains in the prison yard.

Got the picture?

To refuse to offer forgiveness to your offenders is to lock them up in the prison of your heart and to closely monitor them to ensure they don't escape that you also remain where they are. That's imprisonment for both of you.

Take a close look at the Parable of Jesus in Matthew 18:23-35 NIV.

"...the kingdom of heaven is like a king who wanted to settle accounts with his servants. As he be-

gan the settlement, a man who owed him ten thousand bags of gold was brought to him. Since he was not able to pay, the master ordered that he and his wife and his children and all that he had be sold to repay the debt.

"At this the servant fell on his knees before him. 'Be patient with me,' he begged, 'and I will pay back everything.' The servant's master took pity on him, canceled the debt and let him go.

"But when that servant went out, he found one of his fellow servants who owed him a hundred silver coins. He grabbed him and began to choke him. 'Pay back what you owe me!' he demanded.

"His fellow servant fell to his knees and begged him, 'Be patient with me, and I will pay it back.'
"But he refused. Instead, he went off and had the man thrown into prison until he could pay the debt. When the other servants saw what had happened, they were outraged and went and told their master everything that had happened.

"Then the master called the servant in. 'You wicked servant,' he said, 'I canceled all that debt of yours because you begged me to. Shouldn't you have had mercy on your fellow servant just as I had on you?' In anger his master handed him over to the jailers to be tortured, until he should pay back all he owed.

"This is how my heavenly Father will treat each of you unless you forgive your brother or sister from your heart."

Did you notice that the Master also jailed that wicked servant who refused to forgive his colleague? That's how it is with God. If you refuse to forgive your offenders, your heavenly Father too will not forgive you and that implies prison for two.

Now, I know sometimes forgiveness can be so hard to offer depending on the situations surrounding it. But according to Ephesians 4:32, God forgave you for Christ's sake, so you are asked to also forgive for Christ's sake, not for the sake of the offender. That means to be able to forgive, you need to focus your attention on Jesus, not the offence, the hurt or the offender.

And according to Mark 11:25-26, you can't even have a successful prayer life if you don't release your offenders.

You must release your offenders if you desire freedom. There is no freedom for you until you forgive and let go. I didn't say so, Jesus did!

Principle #11

Praying Without Ceasing

'Pray without ceasing' doesn't mean locking yourself up in the room crying to God without going to work or going about your daily business. Rather, it means possessing the consciousness of God's Presence as you go about your daily activities and talking to Him about everything, including your challenges, your results, your clients, your boss, your financial plans, your upcoming business trips, the pain you experienced around your chest before you left home, your fears, your worries and every other detail of your daily life. God wants you to keep discussing these with Him, He's never bored of hearing them!

Proverbs 15:8 and 29 affirm that God is very delighted in our prayers and He hears them. When we pray, we make Him happy because hearing and answering our prayers is one thing He so much enjoys.

Jesus gave a very important illustration to demonstrate the importance of praying without ceasing; that is praying persistently. It's in Luke 18:1-8 BSB. It reads:

'Then Jesus told them a parable about their need to pray at all times and not lose heart: "In a certain town there was a judge who neither feared God nor respected men. And there was a widow in that town who kept appealing to him, 'Give me justice against my adversary.'

For a while he refused, but later he said to himself, 'Though I neither fear God nor respect men, yet because this widow keeps pestering me, I will give her justice. Then she will stop wearing me out with her perpetual requests.'"

And the Lord said, "Listen to the words of the unjust judge. Will not God bring about justice for His elect who cry out to Him day and night? Will He continue to defer their help? I tell you, He will promptly carry out justice on their behalf. Nevertheless, when the Son of Man comes, will He find faith on earth?"

The judge in that parable was described as a wicked man who feared neither God nor respected men, yet because a woman was persistent in her request, He gave her what she wanted. He didn't answer that widow because He was kind, rather he answered her because she wouldn't stop bothering him. How much more our Heavenly Father Who is so delighted in our prayers that He literally invites us with excitement to pray so He can answer us. He said in Jeremiah 33:3 - *"Call to Me, and I will answer you, and show you great and mighty things, which you do not know."*

No matter your level in this Christian race, high or low, you will always need prayers. So get started now; your life depends on it.

Principle #12

Courage

Courage is not the absence of fear, rather it is the mastery of it. Fear comes to all but we don't have to be paralyzed by it. Do what the Psalmist did in Psalm 56:3 the next time you are faced with one - *'What time I am afraid, I will trust in thee'*. That's the way to overcome your fear; put your entire trust in the Lord.

Look at the words the Lord spoke to Joshua during his most fearful moments in Joshua 1:1-9 KJV:

"Now after the death of Moses the servant of the LORD it came to pass, that the LORD spake unto Joshua the son of Nun, Moses' minister, saying, Moses my servant is dead; now therefore arise, go over this Jordan, thou, and all this people, unto the

land which I do give to them, even to the children of Israel. Every place that the sole of your foot shall tread upon, that have I given unto you, as I said unto Moses. From the wilderness and this Lebanon even unto the great river, the river Euphrates, all the land of the Hittites, and unto the great sea toward the going down of the sun, shall be your coast. There shall not any man be able to stand before thee all the days of thy life: as I was with Moses, so I will be with thee: I will not fail thee, nor forsake thee. Be strong and of a good courage: for unto this people shalt thou divide for an inheritance the land, which I sware unto their fathers to give them. Only be thou strong and very courageous, that thou mayest observe to do according to all the law, which Moses my servant commanded thee: turn not from it to the right hand or to the left, that thou mayest prosper whithersoever thou goest. This book of the law shall not depart out of thy mouth; but thou shalt meditate therein day and night, that thou mayest observe to do according to all that is written therein: for then thou shalt make thy way prosperous, and then thou shalt have good success. Have not I commanded thee? Be strong and of a good courage; be not afraid, neither be thou dismayed: for the LORD thy God is with thee whithersoever thou goest."

His Master had just died, and now being the new leader, he became so afraid that God had to encourage him by reassuring him of His abiding presence. And that is where our courage always comes from – God's Abiding Presence.

Nothing gives a man courage more than the consciousness of God's Presence.

Psalm 23: 5 says *"You prepare a table before me in the presence of my enemies. You anoint my head with oil; my cup overflows."*

What can give a man the confidence to enjoy a meal with all his enemies watching? It is the Presence of the Good Shepherd.

So do you need courage to overcome certain challenges or to undertake certain tasks? Talk to God about it. He is the Source of ever flowing courage.

Principle #13

Awareness of God's Goodness

God is good, all the time - regardless of your pains, sorrows, tears, disappointments, failures, ill health, heart aches, losses, and every other unpleasant situation in your life. It is the realization of the goodness of God even in all of these that makes them 'work together for your good'. Never blame God for any of your predicaments!

Psalm 145:9 ESV says: *"The LORD is good to all, and his mercy is over all that he has made."* So, God's goodness is not questionable at all regardless of what is happening to us or around us. And because of the awareness or consciousness of His goodness, we can be sure that everything He allows into our lives is working together for our good.

Romans 8:28 NIV says:

"And we know that in all things God works for the good of those who love him, who have been called according to his purpose."

Let's consider one example from the scriptures to establish this truth.

Look at what happened to Daniel in the text below and how the Lord turned it for his good.

Daniel 6:1-28 KJV:

"It pleased Darius to set over the kingdom an hundred and twenty princes, which should be over the whole kingdom; And over these three presidents; of whom Daniel was first: that the princes might give accounts unto them, and the king should have no damage. Then this Daniel was preferred above the presidents and princes, because an excellent spirit was in him; and the king thought to set him over the whole realm. Then the presidents and princes sought to find occasion against Daniel concerning the kingdom; but they could find none occasion nor fault; forasmuch as he was faithful, neither was there any error or fault found in him. Then said these men, We shall not find any occasion against

this Daniel, except we find it against him concerning the law of his God.

Then these presidents and princes assembled together to the king, and said thus unto him, King Darius, live for ever. All the presidents of the kingdom, the governors, and the princes, the counsellors, and the captains, have consulted together to establish a royal statute, and to make a firm decree, that whosoever shall ask a petition of any God or man for thirty days, save of thee, O king, he shall be cast into the den of lions. Now, O king, establish the decree, and sign the writing, that it be not changed, according to the law of the Medes and Persians, which altereth not. Wherefore king Darius signed the writing and the decree.

Now when Daniel knew that the writing was signed, he went into his house; and his windows being open in his chamber toward Jerusalem, he kneeled upon his knees three times a day, and prayed, and gave thanks before his God, as he did aforetime. Then these men assembled, and found Daniel praying and making supplication before his

God. Then they came near, and spake before the king concerning the king's decree; Hast thou not signed a decree, that every man that shall ask a petition of any God or man within thirty days, save of thee, O king, shall be cast into the den of lions? The king answered and said, The thing is true, according to the law of the Medes and Persians, which altereth not. Then answered they and said before the king, That Daniel, which is of the children of the captivity of Judah, regardeth not thee, O king, nor the decree that thou hast signed, but maketh his petition three times a day.

Then the king, when he heard these words, was sore displeased with himself, and set his heart on Daniel to deliver him: and he laboured till the going down of the sun to deliver him. Then these men assembled unto the king, and said unto the king, Know, O king, that the law of the Medes and Persians is, That no decree nor statute which the king establisheth may be changed.

Then the king commanded, and they brought Daniel, and cast him into the den of lions. Now the king spake and said unto Daniel, Thy God whom thou servest continually, he will deliver thee. And a stone was brought, and laid upon the mouth of the den; and the king sealed it with his own signet, and with the signet of his lords; that the purpose might not be changed concerning Daniel. Then the king went to his palace, and passed the night fasting: neither were instruments of musick brought before him: and his sleep went from him.

Then the king arose very early in the morning, and went in haste unto the den of lions. And when he came to the den, he cried with a lamentable voice unto Daniel: and the king spake and said to Daniel, O Daniel, servant of the living God, is thy God, whom thou servest continually, able to deliver thee from the lions? Then said Daniel unto the king, O king, live for ever. My God hath sent his angel, and hath shut the lions' mouths, that they have not hurt me: forasmuch as before him innocency was found in me; and also before thee, O king, have I done no hurt. Then was the king exceeding glad for him, and commanded that they should take Daniel up out of the den. So Daniel was taken up out of the den, and no manner of hurt was found upon him, because he believed in his God.

And the king commanded, and they brought those men which had accused Daniel, and they cast them into the den of lions, them, their children, and their wives; and the lions had the mastery of them, and brake all their bones in pieces or ever they came at the bottom of the den.

Then king Darius wrote unto all people, nations, and languages, that dwell in all the earth; Peace be multiplied unto you.

I make a decree, That in every dominion of my kingdom men tremble and fear before the God of Daniel: for he is the living God, and stedfast for ever, and his kingdom that which shall not be destroyed, and his dominion shall be even unto the end.

He delivereth and rescueth, and he worketh signs and wonders in heaven and in earth, who hath delivered Daniel from the power of the lions.

So this Daniel prospered in the reign of Darius, and in the reign of Cyrus the Persian."

In that story, Daniel got into trouble simply because he chose to pray to His God. He landed in the Den of Lions and it seemed as if that was the end of his life. That's something anybody would describe as a terrible situation and on-lookers must have been wondering what would become of Daniel.

But because the Lord is a good God, He didn't only deliver Daniel from the power of those lions, He prospered him and used the miracle of his deliverance to draw the entire nation to Himself as reflected in the letter the king sent to his entire kingdom that all men should start worshiping the God of Daniel.

If you love God, you can be assured that all your experiences in life (good and bad) will ultimately work together for your good. They always do.

Principle #14

Your Joy is Your Choice

Joy is not a response to external stimuli, rather it is a CHOICE you make.

If you wait for conditions to be favorable before you decide to be joyful, you may at best be operating at the level of happiness which is very transient.

Nehemiah 8:10 says *'...the joy of the LORD is your strength.'* Meaning weakness is inevitable when the joy of the Lord is absent.

According to the standard of scriptures, we are to rejoice always (in all situations). For instance, 1 Thessalonians 5:16 says *'Rejoice evermore'.*

There's a portion of the Bible I wish to share with you regarding this subject of choosing to be joyful regardless of the happenings in and around us. It's in Habakkuk 3:17-19 BSB:

*"Though the fig tree does not bud
  and no fruit is on the vines,
though the olive crop fails
  and the fields produce no food,
though the sheep are cut off from the fold
  and no cattle are in the stalls,
yet I will exult in the LORD;
  I will rejoice in the God of my salvation!
GOD the Lord is my strength;
  He makes my feet like those of a deer;
  He makes me walk upon the heights!"*

Now, if you take a look at the conditions presented in this text, they do not call for any form of rejoicing at all, at least not in the physical. No fruits, no olive crops, no food, no cattle in the stalls – all typical of failure and emptiness. Yet the writer said *'I will rejoice in the God of my salvation.'*

Notice the object of the rejoicing; 'the

God of my salvation.' So, when it comes to the matter of rejoicing, it's not about what is happening or not happening; it's about the God of your salvation. That's why that Nehemiah 8:10 quoted earlier says the joy of the Lord is your strength. It has to be connected to the Lord for it to be the right rejoicing.

Choose joy regardless of what you face daily. Its joy's absence that leaves you mentally exhausted. Jesus is the Giver of Joy, talk to Him today!

Conclusion

So far, the Lord has revealed some biblical principles to us. The purpose is not just to know, document or preach them, rather they were revealed so that we can walk in them.

According to John 8:32, only the truth that is known sets free. So, go through these principles one by one and determine to build your Christian walk around them for a life of Kingdom impact here on earth.

Jesus said in John 13:17(NLT) - *"You know these things- now do them! That is the path of blessing."*

May the Lord release upon you and your entire household the grace to walk worthy of His calling upon your lives in Jesus Name!

WHY YOU REALLY NEED JESUS!

You might have heard a lot of Preachers talk about the importance of surrendering one's life to Jesus and even the dangers of not doing so at one time or the other without you being really moved. But with these three (3) important reasons highlighted below, I strongly believe you will not need another sermon before deciding to yield to His saving grace regardless of your religious beliefs.

1. **You have an Enemy to overcome:** There is an adversary who is all out to steal from you, kill you and destroy you regardless of your level of education, moral uprightness, societal influence or even religious beliefs. He is Devil by name (John 10:10, 1 Peter 5: 8), and he doesn't release any of

his captives until he completely destroys their souls in hell. The ONLY One Who can deliver you from his manipulations and also save your soul from him is Jesus Christ.

2. **You have an Appointment to keep:** Being alive and reading this implies you have a very important and inevitable appointment to keep. It is an appointment with death (Hebrews 9:27). Death is the sure end of all mortals (of which you are part); and to enable you prepare for this appointment without fear of eternal damnation, you need Jesus. He is the ONLY One Who has power over death (Revelation 1:18).

3. **You have a Judge to face:** Upon departure from this earth, you will have to stand before a judgment throne to render an account of your earthly life (Hebrews 9:27, Romans 14:12). The outcome of this judgment is what will determine your eternal abode which will either be Heaven

or the Lake of fire. Interestingly, the Judge Who will preside over your case and also decide where you will spend your eternity is Jesus (John 5:21-30, 2 Timothy 4:1). I perceive you are thinking "is God not our Judge? Why Jesus?' Well, you are not wrong. But God the Father Himself is the One Who handed over all the judgment to His Son, Jesus Christ. Read the verse 22 of that John chapter 5. So Jesus is the ONLY One Who has the power to either judge you guilty or guiltless in eternity.

Now that you know these, the wisest thing you can do for yourself is to quickly establish a relationship with Jesus, since you don't even know how close your appointment with death is. To do this, say this prayer aloud:

"Lord Jesus, I am a sinner and I cannot help myself. Wash me in your precious blood and make me a new creature. I open the door of my heart to you today, come into my life and become my Lord and Savior. Grant me the grace to overcome the devil, prepare me for eternity

and help me to escape the judgment reserved for sinners. Thank You Jesus for saving me. Amen."

Congratulations! You are now SAVED. Go and sin no more.

To learn more about your new relationship with Jesus, kindly send an Email to info@gloem.org or emancipation4souls@yahoo.com, we will send you a material that will help you. You can also call, text or send whatsapp message to +1 587 9735910 or +1 587 9695910 for further assistance.

And to learn more about God, His Word and His plans for your life, kindly visit our Facebook page [***https://www.facebook.com/gloem.org***] for daily meditation in the Word of God (all year round) and our Blog page [***https://gloem.org/myblog***] for life transforming publications.

You are also invited to listen to Freedom Podcast: The Official Weekly Podcast of Global Emancipation Ministries – Calgary via https://anchor.fm/gloem

All these great resources capable of developing your spiritual stamina will help you become an overcomer in life regardless of what comes your way.

PRAYER POINTS

1. Father, thank You for opening my eyes to the truths contained in this book.
2. Father, please cause every experience in my life to work together for my good.
3. I cancel everything contrary to my prosperity and advancement in Jesus' Name.
4. God of all possibilities, please cause my grass to become green again.
5. From today, my breakthrough shall no longer be delayed in Jesus' Name.
6. Father, beginning from now, please release upon me and my household the ability to walk with you faithfully in the Name of Jesus.
7. Father, I thank You for answering all my prayers. Glory be to Your Holy Name. Hallelujah!

BECOME A FINANCIAL PARTNER WITH JESUS

At *Global Emancipation Ministries - Calgary*, our mandate is *to liberate men through the knowledge of the Truth* and our mission statement is *creating channels through which men can encounter the Truth - [Isaiah 61:1-3; John 8:32, 36; I Thessalonians 5:24]*.

Our Ministerial Activities include Rural and Urban Evangelical Outreaches, Prison Evangelism, Hospital Ministrations, Mobilization for Missions Support, Teaching of the undiluted Word of God, Scripture-Based Seminars, Discipleship, Training of Field Missionaries and Empowerment of underprivileged ones among other Field Ministerial Tasks.

If you sense the Lord is calling you to reach out to the lost by engaging in any of these activities or by assisting those involved with your resources, please feel free to join us. Let us come together as we take the Gospel of our Lord Jesus Christ to the hurting and forgotten ones. [Mark 16:15-20].

Please join us in these kingdom projects by making your weekly, monthly, quarterly or annual donations to Global Emancipation Ministries – Calgary.

You can visit the "GIVE" section on our website, www.gloem.org, to learn about the ways to give.

For acknowledgement, please advise your donations to us by email: info@gloem.org or emancipation4souls@yahoo.com, and kindly include your details i.e. name, address, email and location. Alternatively, you can simply call +1 587 9735910 to do same.

You can also volunteer your gifts and talents in the service of the Lord through our ministerial platforms regardless of your location. To get information on how to go about this, please visit www.gloem.org and contact us via email: info@gloem.org or emancipation4souls@yahoo.com.

God bless you.

About the Author

By the special grace of God, **Anthony O. Adefarakan** is the privileged President of **Global Emancipation Ministries - Calgary (GLOEM)** with headquarters in Canada, North America and **Emancipating Truth Ministry International (ETMI)** with headquarters in Nigeria, West Africa.

The Lord called him into the field ministry in February 2008 with the mandate to liberate men through the knowledge of the Truth, and by December 2012 he was ordained and commissioned as the Pioneer Pastor – in – Charge of The Redeemed Christian Church of God, Revelation Parish, Shalom Area under Delta Province III, Nigeria where he served until 1st February 2015 when he officially handed over to a new Pastor in order to focus on his field ministry to which the Lord had earlier called him and for which the authority of the church had already prayed and released him to undertake.

On 29th September 2013, he was awarded a Post Graduate Diploma in Tent – Making Mission from the Redeemed Christian School of Missions, Nigeria (RECSOM, Asaba Campus) where he also had the privilege to train Pastors and Missionaries as a lecturer in 2017.

Since the commissioning of his field ministry in 2015 he has had the opportunity to lead his ministry officers to field ministrations in different Prisons, Hospitals, Orphanages, Rural communities, Camp settlements, Markets, Local churches among other places with great successes on all occasions – such as salvation of sinners, healing of the sick, financial empowerment of mission churches, provision of relief materials to the poor, provision of medical services to the underprivileged, baptism in the Holy Ghost, deliverance from demonic oppression, release of inmates just to mention a few - all to the glory of God Who alone is the Doer.

He is the author of other best-selling titles such as *The Law of Kinds, Learning From the Ants, The Immutability of God's Counsel, Surely there is an End, Life Applicable lessons from the Book of Ruth, One thing is Needful Weekly Devotional Guide, Life Applicable Revelations from God's Word* (Volumes 1 and 2) among others.

He is blissfully married to Ifeoluwa A. Adefarakan and their marriage is fruitful to the glory of God.

Jesus is his Message, Freedom is the Outcome!
Isaiah 61:1-3

www.ingramcontent.com/pod-product-compliance
Lightning Source LLC
Chambersburg PA
CBHW021431070526
44577CB00001B/157